EARTH SCIENCE LIBRARY
VOLCANOES AND EARTHQUAKES

MARTYN BRAMWELL

Franklin Watts

London · New York · Toronto · Sydney

© 1986 Franklin Watts

First published in Great Britain by
Franklin Watts
12a Golden Square
London W1

First published in the USA by
Franklin Watts Inc.
387 Park Avenue South
New York, N.Y. 10016

First published in Australia by
Franklin Watts Australia
14 Mars Road
Lane Cove
NSW 2066

UK ISBN: 0 86313 409 2
US ISBN: 0-531-10177-0
Library of Congress Catalog Card
No: 85-52045

Printed in Belgium

Designed by Ben White

Picture research by Mick
Alexander

Illustrations:
Chris Forsey
Hayward Art Group
Colin Newman/Linden Artists

Photographs:
Ardea 10, 18, 23r
Bruce Coleman 23l
Susan Griggs 29
GeoScience Features back cover, 10r, 16, 19b, 27
Robert Harding 9
Frank Lane 1, 4, 10l, 14, 15, 25, 26
Natural Science Photos 21
John Reader 20
Woodmansterne 12, 17, 19t
ZEFA 13, 22

acc. 81-79

EARTH SCIENCE LIBRARY

VOLCANOES AND EARTHQUAKES

MARTYN BRAMWELL

Contents

The violent earth

Every year several hundred earthquakes and volcanic **eruptions** shake the surface of our planet. Luckily, most of them occur under the deep oceans or in places where not many people live. But once every few years a major earthquake or eruption hits a heavily populated area. The result is usually a disaster that makes world headlines.

In 1985 there were two. In September a big earthquake struck Mexico City – one of the world's most crowded cities. Thousands died and tens of thousands were left homeless. And just two months later, in the mountains of Colombia, the eruption of Nevado del Ruiz buried the town of Armero beneath an avalanche of volcanic mud.

▽ Fountains of molten rock, or **lava**, burst from a **crater** rim on one of the volcanic islands of Hawaii. Glowing lava pours into a lava lake filling the circular crater. The sky is darkened by clouds of dust and gas.

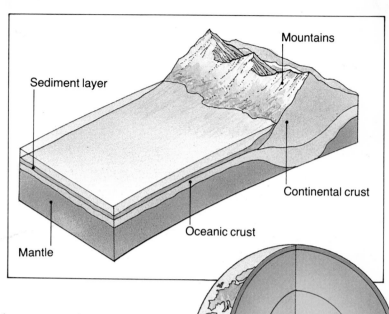

▷ The rocks of the crust are rather like rafts, floating on top of the mantle layer. Continental crust is about 35 km (22 miles) thick on average, but it is up to 70 km (43 miles) thick beneath mountain ranges. Oceanic crust forms a much more even layer, averaging 6 km (3½ miles) thick. The deep sea bed is covered with fine muddy **sediments** made mainly of the shells of tiny drifting sea animals.

Volcanoes and earthquakes are as impressive to us as they were to our ancestors. But today we understand a lot more about them. By studying volcanic rocks and gases, and the shock waves caused by earthquakes, geologists have learned a great deal about the earth's interior.

The thin hard surface layer, called the **crust**, is made of two main types of rock. The continents are made of light **granite**-type rocks and these float, like huge rafts, on the denser rocks below. The continental rocks are very ancient. Some are more than 3,500 million years old. The crust beneath the oceans is made of heavier rock. It is much thinner, and also very much younger. Nowhere is it more than 200 million years old.

Below the crust lies the thick **mantle** layer. It is neither true solid nor true liquid, but is more like a thick paste – very hot and always moving, driven by the heat inside the earth. Deeper still lies the **core**, made up mainly of iron. Its outer part is liquid, and movements inside it produce the earth's magnetic field. The innermost part of the core is solid.

△ A cross-section through the earth reveals that it has four main layers. Volcanoes occur where hot molten rock from the mantle layer bursts through the thin crust on to the surface.

Inside a volcano

The thick, hot, molten rock of the upper mantle is called **magma**. It lies just a few miles beneath our feet, and in some parts of the world it forces its way right up through the crust. When it reaches the surface, it is called lava.

The enormous pressure deep in the crust keeps most of the magma fairly solid. But as it rises, it becomes more liquid. More and more of its minerals melt. Pieces of crustal rock are dissolved in it too, adding their own minerals to the constantly changing chemical "soup." The result of all this mixing is that one big reservoir of magma may eventually produce a wide range of very different rock types.

When magma reaches the surface, it erupts from a hole or **vent**, sometimes oozing out steadily, sometimes blasting out with incredible violence. However, not all the magma gets that far. Some cools and hardens inside the crust, producing **sills** and **dykes** and other features.

▽ Molten rock rising from a magma chamber does not always reach the earth's surface. Some forces its way between layers of crustal rocks or into cracks in the rock layers. When the magma cools and hardens like this, the new rock is called an "igneous intrusion." **Intrusive** means "forced in." We call this whole family of rocks the **igneous rocks**, meaning rocks "born of fire."

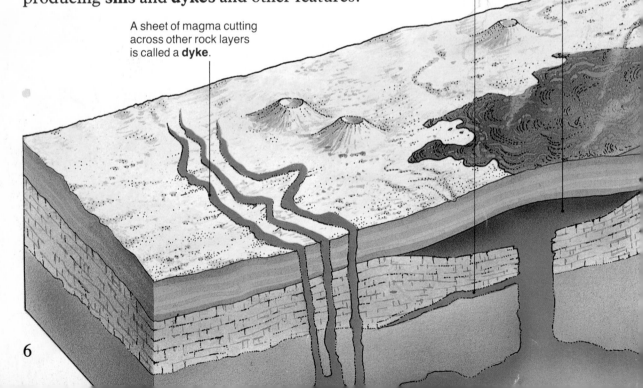

Large lens-shaped masses of cooled magma are called **laccoliths**.

Magma forced in between layers of other rock is called a **sill**.

A sheet of magma cutting across other rock layers is called a **dyke**.

▽ When a volcano erupts, clouds of **ash**, gas and vapor are hurled into the atmosphere. The "ash" conists of tiny pieces of lava. When it falls to earth, it hardens into a rock called tuff. As well as the main pipe and vent, a volcano may have one or more side vents. Tuffs and lavas are called "**extrusive** rocks." The word means "forced out."

Magma reaches the surface through the main **pipe** of a volcano. The opening is called the **vent**.

Magma starts its upward journey from a **magma chamber** in the upper mantle.

Earth's wandering continents

The shapes of the continents have intrigued people for centuries. One constant puzzle was the close match of the shapes of South America and Africa, separated by the Atlantic Ocean.

Between 1858 and 1915 several scientists suggested that the two continents had once been joined together. But no one could explain how they had split apart. The idea was dismissed as being too far-fetched. But in the 1960s the key to the puzzle was found, deep beneath the Atlantic Ocean.

Scientists studying the sea bed discovered that magma was rising to the surface all along a huge submarine mountain range running down the middle of the ocean. They also found that the sea bed was moving away from the ridge at each side, as if carried on huge conveyor belts. But the earth is not getting bigger. If new crust appears in one place, it must disappear somewhere else.

The scientists then went to the Pacific Ocean and looked at the deep **trenches** lying off western South America and the islands of Southeast Asia. The pattern fitted. Here, old ocean crust was being dragged back down into the mantle. A new theory was born. It was called "**plate tectonics.**" The crust was no longer thought of as a single solid shell but as a jigsaw puzzle of separate pieces, all on the move.

The final question was "How?," and the answer again lay in the mantle. We now know that the mantle is more active in some places than in others, and that in those areas it is churning over like a pan of simmering porridge. Currents within the mantle power the "conveyor belts," and these in turn carry the continental rafts along.

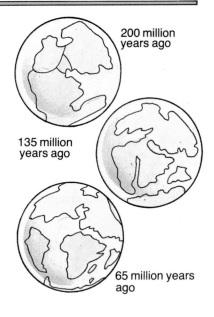

200 million years ago

135 million years ago

65 million years ago

△ Scientists can measure the present speed of plate movements and use computers to plot where the continents were millions of years ago.

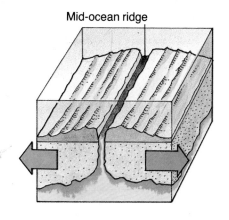

Mid-ocean ridge

◁ As new magma rises to the surface, it hardens into new oceanic crust and is carried outward by the "conveyor belts."

▷ When the moving oceanic plate "hits" a continent, it is dragged down under the land mass. The rocks melt again and fuel the active volcanoes in the mountains above.

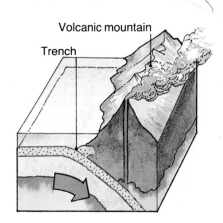

Volcanic mountain

Trench

▷ The "Ring of Fire," shown in red on the map, is the active zone around the Pacific Ocean where plates of ocean crust plunge under the land. Most of the world's big earthquakes and volcanoes are concentrated here. The blue lines show the plate edges. Those in mid-ocean are where new crust is being formed. The blue lines in Asia are old collision zones.

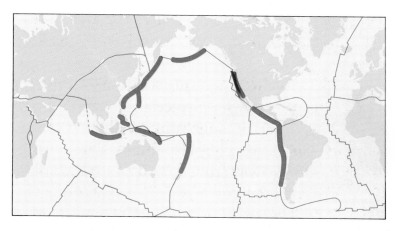

◁ The towering peaks of the Andes Mountains rise through the clouds near Cuzco in Peru. The mountains were built by the crushing and squeezing of the rocks of the South American plate, where a large slab of Pacific Ocean floor dives beneath it. As the sea bed crust is dragged deep into the earth, it melts, feeding molten rock into the volcanoes scattered along the mountain chain. And as the oceanic plate goes down, it drags against the continental rocks, causing frequent earthquakes.

The shape of a volcano and the way it behaves in an eruption depend on the chemistry of the lava, on how "runny" it is, and on how much gas there is in it. There are two main types of lavas – very dark **basalt**-type lavas which are usually found where the crust is splitting apart, and much stiffer, light-colored lavas which are found where crustal plates are coming together. Here we take a closer look at the basalt types of volcanoes.

Because these volcanoes are typical of areas where new crust is being formed, most of them are found under the oceans. They also occur where islands poke out of the sea directly over very active parts of the earth's crust. Some of the most spectacular eruptions of this type occur on the islands of Hawaii – sitting over what geologists call a "hot spot" on the Pacific Ocean bed. Similar types of eruption have happened on Iceland and the small islands nearby, all of which sit on the

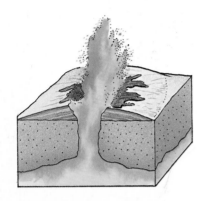

△ The typical shape of a basalt-type volcano is a low, flat dome with extensive thin lava flows spreading out all around it. Because the runny lava spreads so quickly, the dome does not build up to any great height.

◁ This strange landscape is the surface of a recent flow of lava from Kilauea volcano on the Hawaiian island of Kauai. As the lava spread out, its upper surface started to cool and harden while the lava below remained hot and runny. The result is a wrinkled surface called ropy lava. Its Hawaiian name is "**pahoehoe**." Thicker, less runny basalt lava breaks into rough cinder-like pieces and is called "**aa**."

northern arm of the great mid-Atlantic mountain chain.

If the lava wells up steadily through a big crack in the crust, the gas inside it has time to escape gently. The lava spills out and spreads over a wide area. In the past such "flood basalts" have covered thousands of square miles. But if the vent is small, or blocked, so that the lava is kept under pressure, the gas cannot escape. When the vent finally blows clear, the gas explodes, spraying fountains of glowing lava droplets hundreds of feet into the air.

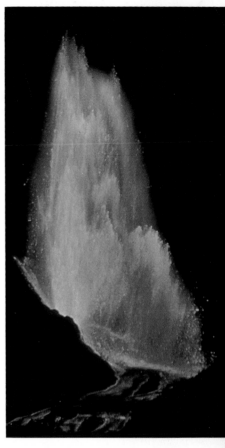

△ The volcano of Kilauea puts on a spectacular fire fountain display during a night eruption. Some of the gas explosions hurl showers of lava droplets 350 m (1,150 ft) into the air.

◁ A Hawaiian geologist stands on the hardened crust of a lava flow. His telescopic pole is used to measure the lava thickness. Beneath his feet, red-hot lava is still flowing through a natural tunnel which will remain long after the lava has cooled and hardened.

Ash, gas and pasty lava

The second main group of lavas are much lighter in color because they contain large amounts of **silica**. Instead of flowing easily, these lavas are very stiff and pasty. The gases trapped in them cannot escape easily, so the lavas are highly explosive. They also tend to harden in the pipe of the volcano, blocking the outlet until the pressure builds up to a point where the entire top of the volcano may be blown off.

This type of volcano is typical of areas where crustal plates are moving toward each other so that one is being forced down into the earth and destroyed.

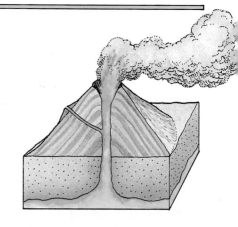

△ The typical shape of a strato-volcano is a high, steep-sided cone built up of layer upon layer of ash and lava.

▷ Cotopaxi is one of the most beautiful peaks in the Andes, rising 5,897 m (19,500 ft) high in the mountains of Ecuador. It is one of the highest volcanoes in the world, and its frequent eruptions have caused widespread damage.

▽ Clad in heat-reflecting insulated suits, Italian scientists lower a probe into one of the side vents of Mount Etna to obtain samples of the gases being released.

The volcanoes are common in young mountain chains like the Andes, and in island arcs like those of Japan, the Philippines and the northern Pacific. The volcanoes themselves are usually steep-sided cones, formed of alternating layers of lava and ash. They are called strato-volcanoes and include some of the world's most beautiful mountains – Cotopaxi in the Andes, Fuji in Japan and Vesuvius in Italy.

These strato-volcanoes are the most destructive of all. In AD 79 Vesuvius erupted violently, burying the town of Pompeii in ash. The nearby port of Herculaneum was completely engulfed in an avalanche of mud and waterlogged volcanic ash. But the most deadly eruption of all is the "nuée ardente," meaning "glowing cloud." This happens when the side of a blocked volcano is blown out, releasing a dense cloud of red-hot ash and gas which surges down the mountain, destroying everything in its path.

In 1902 Mt. Pelée on the island of Martinique erupted in this way. In the space of just a few minutes the town of St. Pierre and its 30,000 inhabitants were engulfed. There were just two survivors.

▷ For several years the north side of Mount St. Helens had been bulging. Parts of the mountain had risen by 100 m (33 ft) in less than a year. When the mountain gave way, the sideways blast flattened the surrounding forest and killed several people working and camping in the area.

Thousands of animals were killed, and all plant life was wiped out by the blast, the avalanches of mud which followed, and the choking dust which later settled over the area. Yet just three years later, scientists found seedlings pushing up through the ash. The process of recovery had begun.

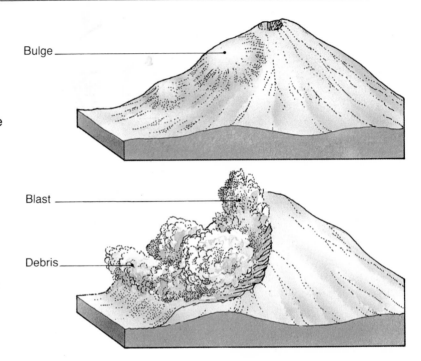

Bulge

Blast

Debris

At 8.32 on the morning of May 18, 1980 a huge volcanic eruption blew the top 400 m (1,320 ft) off Mount St. Helens in the Cascade mountains of Washington. A column of dust, ash and gas climbed more than 19 km (12 miles) into the sky. Nearly 400 sq km (155 sq miles) of forest were completely flattened by the blast, and towns up to 500 km (310 miles) down-wind were covered in gritty volcanic ash.

The eruption itself was not unexpected. Geologists had been studying the mountain for several years, drilling rock samples from the 40,000-year-old cone and measuring the frequent small earthquakes coming from beneath it. In the mid-1970s they predicted an eruption sometime before the year 2000. What took them all by surprise was the suddenness and staggering force of the explosion when it came.

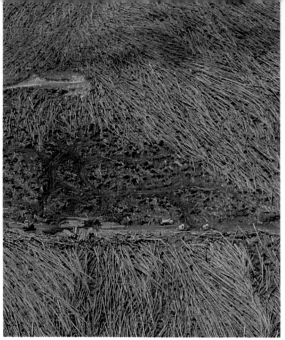

△ The force of the eruption is clear from this view of the gaping crater left behind. Millions of tons of solid rock were blasted into dust. Some of it was thrown so high that it is still drifting in the upper atmosphere.

△ In the words of a pilot flying over the scene, the forest below looked as if "some giant had just combed his hair." Here, foresters begin the enormous job of salvaging what they can of the valuable timber.

Mount St. Helens had been quiet since its last eruption in 1857, but in the 1970s small-scale earthquakes became more and more frequent – a sure sign that magma was rising beneath the mountain. The northern slope developed a prominent bulge as the ancient layers of ash and lava were forced upwards by the thick pasty lava rising from below. When the side of the mountain finally gave way, the searing blast of hot gas, rock and lava stripped the countryside in its path, leaving a desert of hot gray ash.

The volcano continued erupting for four days and then fell quiet. On May 25, there was another big eruption, but although the volcano erupted several times more during the following months, the main force was spent. Mount St. Helens had blown its top. It should now remain peaceful for another 50 to 150 years.

The birth and death of islands

In 1961 the tiny volcanic island of Tristan da Cunha erupted. Its entire population of about 260 people had to be evacuated. It was the first time most people had ever heard of the island, for it is one of the most remote of all British territories – perched on the mid-ocean ridge in the far south of the Atlantic Ocean.

In 1963 the world's newspapers and television cameras were focusing on events at the opposite end of the great Atlantic mountain chain. This time the action lay 32 km (20 miles) southwest of Iceland where, in the space of a day, a new island was born. Clouds of ash and steam rose above the waves as huge submarine explosions churned and shook the sea. Then, as the growing tip of the island broke the surface, bright red lava poured from dozens of vents in the black cone of ash. The

△ Just after midnight on January 23, 1973 a new volcano, Eldjfell, burst into life on the island of Heimaey, just off the coast of Iceland. In less than an hour a large crack had split the ground and lava was fountaining from dozens of vents, partially burying the main town of Westmannaeyjar.

▷ The birth of an island. Billowing clouds of ash and steam hang over one of the lava vents on the new island of Surtsey.

island was named Surtsey. Two years later it had grown to more than 2.5 km (1½ miles) across and was already being colonized by plants, insects and birds.

After spending a year in Britain, the people of Tristan da Cunha returned to their distant island home. Perhaps some time in the future people will live on Surtsey – or on bigger, as yet unborn, islands on the North Atlantic Ridge.

But volcanic activity can destroy land as well as create it. The biggest eruption witnessed in historical times occurred in 1883, when the island of Krakatau, between Java and Sumatra, was torn apart by a series of explosions that were heard more than 4,800 km (3,000 miles) away in Australia. It is estimated that 36,000 people died as huge **tsunamis** ("tidal waves") struck coastal villages throughout the region. Only three small fragments of the island remained after the eruption, and they were stripped of life. Yet 50 years later the islands were once again clothed in forest.

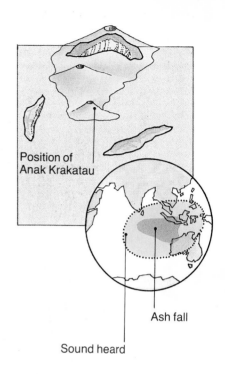

Position of Anak Krakatau

Ash fall

Sound heard

△ When Krakatau was destroyed, only three small fragments (shown in green) were left. But in 1927 a new island appeared. It was named Anak Krakatau – Child of Krakatau.

Echoes of the past

We sometimes use expressions like "as solid as a rock" and "as old as the hills," but we can say this only because our own lifespan is so short. The physical world around us seems permanent only because it changes so very slowly. But change it does. No sooner has a mountain range started to rise above the surrounding land than wind and rain, rivers and glaciers start to wear it away, sweeping the debris down to the sea.

   The beautiful conical peaks of volcanoes suffer the same fate – but rather more quickly. And even the igneous rocks that have solidified deep inside the crust will some day reappear at the earth's surface when all the overlying rock layers have been stripped away.

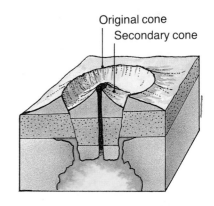

Original cone
Secondary cone

▽ Crater Lake, in Oregon, today fills the huge **caldera**, or crater, formed when the upper part of the original volcano collapsed into the magma chamber below.

Because igneous rocks are usually much harder than sedimentary rocks like sandstone, shale and chalk, they wear away more slowly. As a result, ancient volcanoes, lava flows and intrusions often form distinctive landscape features when they are exposed at the earth's surface.

Lava that hardened in the pipe of a long-dead volcano may be left standing like a natural tower when the rest of the volcano has gone. Basalt dykes jut out of the landscape like man-made walls, sometimes radiating outwards like the spokes of a wheel from the core of a long-vanished volcano. The prominent ridge of the Great Whin Sill in northern England gave such a good view over the surrounding area that Hadrian built his famous wall along its crest.

Even the deepest intrusions are exposed in time. The huge granite domes of Yosemite National Park in California and the high moors of Devon and Cornwall in England are formed by the tops of vast granite intrusions whose bases lie at some unknown depth.

△ The 80-m (260-ft) high pillar of rock dominating the French town of Le Puy was once the central pipe of a volcano.

▷ Fingal's Cave in Scotland is carved out of a basalt lava flow. The outer parts cooled quickly into a jumbled mass of rock, but the inner part cooled slowly into tall six-sided columns.

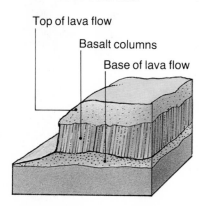

Top of lava flow

Basalt columns

Base of lava flow

Buried treasures

People have lived in the shadow of volcanoes for millions of years, and this simple fact produced one of the most amazing archaeological finds ever made. In the late 1970s archaeologists working at a place called Laetoli in northern Tanzania discovered a series of thin beds of volcanic ash in which there were thousands of animal footprints. But an even bigger surprise lay in store.

In one of the ash layers the scientists found footprints that were clearly human in origin. Three-and-a-half million years ago three people, probably a man leading a woman and child, had crossed this African landscape, leaving their footprints locked forever in the fine damp ash thrown out by the volcano Sadiman, erupting about 30 km (16 miles) to the east.

▽ The Laetoli footprints captured a moment in Africa's distant past when early humans fled from an eruption. Their tracks are crossed by those of a tiny primitive three-toed horse and its foal.

△ Hillside terraces in the Canary Islands increase the amount of agricultural land available to farmers. Volcanic ash is mixed with the soil to help retain the moisture from dew and from the infrequent rainfall.

△ The yellow mineral sulfur is used in the manufacture of many products, including dyes, pesticides, medicines and sulfuric acid. It is also used to vulcanize rubber to make it stronger and more flexible for use in vehicle tires.

The fact that volcanoes can erupt violently has not discouraged people from living close to them. Volcanoes have their good points too, and one of the most important is the rich soils they can produce. The basalt lava flows that spread across southern India millions of years ago produced the fertile black soils of the Deccan Plateau, where much of the world's cotton is now grown. Even the soils of younger, still-active volcanoes can be used. Their soils are usually thinner and less fertile, but they still produce good farmland. In the Mediterranean region the sunny slopes are ideal for vine-growing. On dry volcanic islands like the Canary Islands the soil is terraced to hold the rainwater and is then planted with food crops. And throughout Asia, terraces are used to create rice-fields on steep volcanic slopes.

Finally there is the mineral wealth of the volcanic rocks. The high temperatures, high pressures, melting and mixing that accompany volcanic activity concentrate valuable minerals in veins and cavities and high-grade ores. Copper, sulfur, nickel and bauxite (the source of aluminum) are among the important raw materials mined from volcanic rocks.

Geysers and mud pools

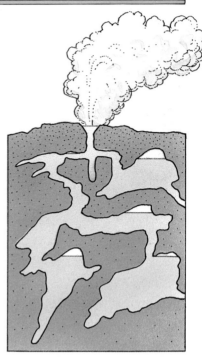

The intense heat of the earth's interior comes closer to the surface at Yellowstone National Park than anywhere else on earth. Here, high in the Rocky Mountains of Wyoming, geologists have measured temperatures well over 200°C only 75 m (250 ft) below ground. In the midst of some of North America's most beautiful mountain scenery this 750,000-year-old caldera floor contains more than 10,000 **geysers**, mud pools and hot mineral springs.

At intervals ranging from a few minutes to almost a day, geysers send their columns of boiling water hissing 50 or 60 m (150–200ft) into the air. Some of the pools are crystal clear and the water is hot enough to cook in. Others are stained brilliant yellow, blue or green by the algae that live in the scalding water. In between are areas of mud pools, where the pink-gray mud heaves and

△ The ground beneath a geyser is honeycombed with chambers and connecting passages. Water seeping through the ground is heated to near boiling point. Steam trapped in the chambers builds up pressure until the water is forced out at the surface. There is then a quiet phase while the pressure builds up again. Castle Geyser (*left*), erupts every 8 hours, spouting near-boiling water 25 m (80 ft) high.

bubbles – each "plop" giving off a strong smell of sulfur as the bubble bursts.

The spectacular displays of Yellowstone are rivaled only by those of Iceland and the North Island of New Zealand. But areas of hot springs are also found in many other parts of the world, including Turkey, Morocco, Japan, East Africa and Kamchatka in the USSR.

Fountaining geysers and shimmering mineral formations are natural tourist attractions. Yellowstone Park alone has more than two million visitors each year. But these regions of **geothermal** energy have another, even more important economic value. In America, Japan, Wairakei in New Zealand and Larderello in Italy, high-pressure, high-temperature steam from the upper crustal rocks is tapped and used to drive electricity-generating turbines.

▽ The geothermal power station at Wairakei on the North Island of New Zealand pipes natural high-pressure steam direct to its generator turbines.

◁ The white crystalline terrace formations at Pamukkale in Turkey are made of travertine – a form of limestone that is deposited from the water as it spills from ledge to ledge.

Tremors and earthquakes

When rocks are squeezed under great pressure, especially when they are heated at the same time, they can bend and fold without breaking, like modelling clay. But if the pressure builds up too quickly, the rocks start to bend under the stress. Then they break – releasing the pent-up energy just as an archer releases the energy in a tightly drawn bow. Shock waves surge through the ground, sometimes for a few seconds, occasionally for several minutes. The results can be devastating.

Frequent small tremors are usually felt in the weeks or months before a volcano erupts. They are caused by the magma forcing its way up through the rocks below. Earthquakes of this type also occur throughout the mid-ocean ridge system where new crust is being formed. However, most of the worst earthquakes are caused by movements at destructive plate margins.

■ Earthquake zones

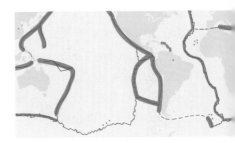

△ The three main zones of earthquake activity. One is closely matched to the "Ring of Fire" around the Pacific. Another follows the mid-ocean ridges where new crust is forming. The third follows the old "collision" line between the African and Indian plates and the huge Eurasian plate.

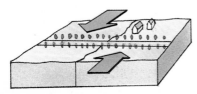

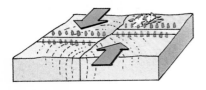

△ Stress builds up until the rocks fracture, sending out shock waves in all directions.

▷ The San Andreas fault cuts a deep gash across the California desert.

△ Houses in Anchorage lie wrecked and half buried after a huge earthquake hit Alaska in 1964.

As one plate is dragged down beneath another, great frictional forces build up. This energy is released in what geologists call "shallow focus" earthquakes, that is, earthquakes starting in the upper 70 km (45 miles) of the crust. It was this type of earthquake that ravaged Mexico City in September 1985.

In other places crustal plates are sliding past each other rather than dipping down. The 960-km (860-mile) long San Andreas **fault** in California marks the line where one of the Pacific plates slides past the North American plate. The fault normally moves about 1 cm ($\frac{1}{4}$ in) a year, releasing the stresses in thousands of small tremors that do no damage. But occasionally the plates "stick." The stress builds up to a critical level and is then released in a major earthquake like the one that destroyed much of the city of San Francisco in 1906.

Measuring and predicting

For many years scientists have been trying to find ways of predicting earthquake and volcanic eruptions so that in times of danger people can be evacuated to safety. There are usually clear signs that a volcano is becoming active. The big problem is to predict just *when* it is likely to erupt.

In all parts of the world people living close to volcanoes have developed their own ways of predicting eruptions, based on the behavior of animals and birds or on the changing sounds made by the volcano itself. More scientific methods rely mainly on two instruments – the **seismometer**, which measures earth tremors, and the **tiltmeter**, which is used to detect changes in the slope of the side of a volcano as magma pushes up from below.

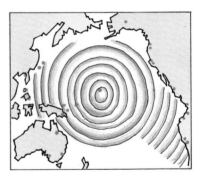

△ Shock waves from an underwater earthquake near Hawaii are picked up by seismic stations all round the Pacific. A central station can then predict when the spreading tsunami (blue) will hit any particular town or city on the coast.

Predicting earthquakes is much more difficult. The seismometer provides a continuous record of even the smallest tremors, and scientists are looking for ways of predicting earthquakes by analyzing the patterns of tremors in areas of high risk.

One form of prediction, however, is proving much more successful. By comparing readings from widely spaced stations, the exact position of an earthquake's origin can be pinpointed, and this has provided an effective early warning system for tsunamis in the Pacific.

Tsunamis are huge surges of water caused by underwater earthquakes or eruptions. Out in mid-ocean they are not very impressive. The waves may be only 1 m (3 ft) high and are often spaced up to 150 km (90 miles) apart. But they travel at up to 800 km/h (500 mph). When the surge hits shallow coastal waters the waves can rear up to 35 m (115 ft) high. They crash inland, causing enormous damage to coastal towns and devastating large areas of farmland.

△ Fishing boats stranded after a tsunami hit the Alaskan port of Seward in March 1964.

▷ Portable seismic units consisting of detector (left) and analyzer are used for studying individual volcanoes.

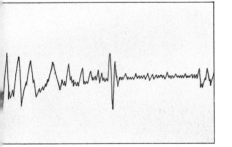

Artificial earthquakes

Once scientists had learned how to analyze the shock waves from natural earthquakes, the next step was to see how the same methods could be used by geologists and engineers. In the search for oilfields, coalfields and deposits of minerals, geologists need to know the thickness of rock layers underground, and whether they are bent into folds or broken by faults.

To obtain this information, shock waves are started by firing an explosive charge in a borehole. Strings of detectors, called **geophones**, are laid out at varying distances from the explosion. The shock waves are recorded as they bounce back from the rock layers below. Computers turn the geophone signals into a printout of the underground geological structures.

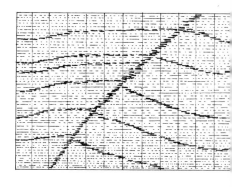

△ Seismic surveying, using man-made shock waves, provides the geologist with an overall "X-ray" picture of a large area. It is used by oil and mining companies, by **hydrologists** looking for new water supplies, and by engineers looking for suitable sites for heavy structures like dams and skyscrapers.

Seismic survey on land

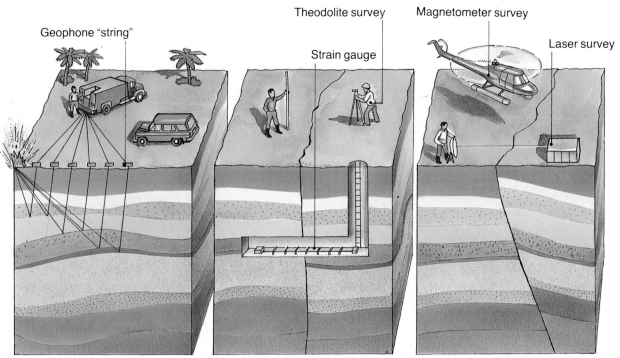

Geophone "string"

Theodolite survey

Strain gauge

Magnetometer survey

Laser survey

▷ A plume of sand spurts from a bore-hole as the explosive charge is fired during a seismic survey in the southern part of Saudi Arabia.

▽ Seismic surveys are often carried out at sea. Explosive charges may be dropped overboard, or shock waves may be created by the discharge of a high-pressure gas "gun" lowered into the sea.

Seismic survey at sea

Geophone "string"

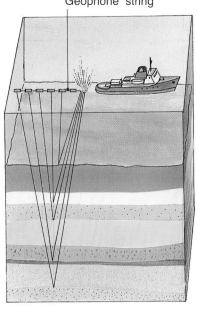

Geologists today use several different methods of "looking" inside the earth. Sensitive **magnetometers** are carried by airborne survey teams looking for iron-rich minerals. These instruments measure tiny variations in the earth's magnetic field. Large deposits of iron ore, for example, show up as unusually high readings. **Gravimeters** are used in much the same way to plot variations in the "pull" of gravity. Dense rocks and minerals like ore deposits cause high readings. Large masses of light material, such as salt, show up as low readings.

Laser beams can now be used to detect even the slightest movements in rocks at either side of a fault. Strain gauges are also used to measure earth movements. They are cemented into place in long tunnels bored through solid rock and can measure the stretching or crushing forces within the rocks. Each new scientific advance increases our understanding of the earth. Together they should help us to use its resources more wisely.

Glossary

Aa   The Hawaiian name for lava that breaks up into rough cinder-like blocks.

Ash   Volcanic ash consists of very fine pieces of lava, less than 4 mm ($\frac{1}{4}$ in) across, blown into the air during an eruption. Larger pieces are called "lapilli."

Basalt   A dark igneous rock that occurs as lava flows and intrusions. It sometimes contains "geodes" (cavities) filled with beautiful crystals.

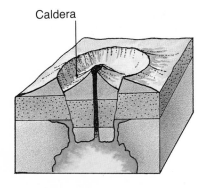

Caldera

Caldera   A huge circular crater, caused when a volcano collapses into the magma chamber below.

Core   The central part of the earth. It consists mainly of iron, with some silicon and sulfur.

Crater   The circular funnel-shaped opening in the top of a volcanic cone.

Crust   The outer solid skin of the earth. If you drew a 10-cm (4-in) diameter circle, and let that represent the earth, the

entire thickness of the crust would fall within the thickness of the pencil line!

Dyke   An intrusive rock formation that cuts across the existing rock layers. Magma is usually intruded, or squeezed, along a line of weakness such as a fault.

Earthquake   A violent shaking of the crustal rocks caused by the rocks breaking under stress or by molten rock forcing its way through them. The most severe quake of recent times was the one that hit Alaska in 1964.

Eruption   The pouring out of lava and gas on to the earth's surface.

Extrusive   Means "forced out" and is used for all lava, ash and gas thrown out in a volcanic eruption.

Fault   A break or fracture running through layers of rock. Faults can be microscopic, occurring in single crystals, or

run for hundreds of miles through the crust.

Geophone   A sensitive instrument, rather like a microphone, used for picking up vibrations in the ground.

Geothermal   Anything to do with the natural heat of the earth's interior.

Geyser   A natural fountain of hot water and steam. The name comes from the Icelandic word "geysir" meaning spouter.

Granite   A light-colored intrusive rock composed mainly of silica (quartz), feldspar and dark mica. Granite often occurs as enormous igneous intrusions.

Gravimeter   An instrument for making extremely fine measurements of the force of gravity at different points on the earth's surface.

Hydrology   The study of water movements on, and under, the earth's surface.

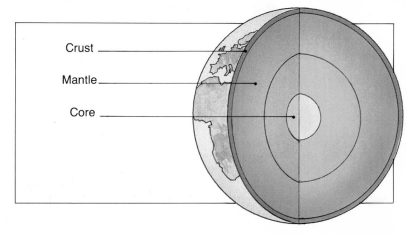

Crust

Mantle

Core

Igneous rocks   All the rock types formed by volcanic activity, both on the surface and deep inside the crust.

Intrusive   Means "forced in" and is used to describe rocks formed when magma is forced in among other rocks.

Laccolith   A large lens-shaped intrusion of solidified magma.

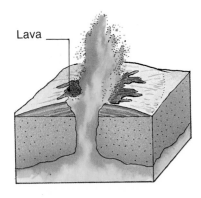

Lava

Lava   Molten rock poured out at the earth's surface. It can be thick and sticky or runny.

Magma   The molten rock deep in the mantle and lower crust, from which igneous rocks are made.

Magnetometer   Scientific instrument for measuring the strength of the earth's magnetic field. It is used in the search for iron-rich materials.

Mantle   The thick layer of semi-molten rock that lies beneath the crust. Movements in the mantle cause the crustal plates to move over the earth's surface.

Pahoehoe   The Hawaiian name for rope-like lava.

Pipe   The vertical or near-vertical passage through which magma rises to the surface.

Plate tectonics   The name given to the theory that the earth's crust is made up of moving sections or "plates."

Sedimentary rocks   Rocks like sandstone, mudstone and chalk, formed when particles of eroded rock material, or the remains of marine animals, pile up on the sea bed and later turn into rock.

Seismology   The study of earthquakes and earthquake shock waves.

Seismometer   A sensitive instrument that detects and records vibrations in the earth's rocks. They may be caused by earthquakes, volcanic eruptions or by scientists setting off explosions during a seismic survey.

Silica   The most common mineral in the earth's crust and the main ingredient of sandstone and granite.

Sill   A thin sheet of intrusive rock forced between other layers of rock.

Tiltmeter   An instrument for measuring minute changes in the slope of the ground. Two containers of liquid are joined by a tube. The liquid levels are noted. If the ground tilts, liquid runs from one container to the other and the liquid levels are altered.

Trench   A long narrow deep area in the ocean, usually close to the edge of a continent or an arc of islands. It marks the zone where the ocean crust is being pulled down into the earth.

Tsunami   An enormous and very destructive sea wave caused by a submarine earthquake or volcanic eruption. Tsunamis are often called "tidal waves," but they have nothing to do with tides.

Vent   Any hole through which lava or gas reaches the surface. If the vent is actively pouring out hot vapor, it is called a "fumarole."

Volcano   A mountain or hill with a central pipe through which lava, ash and gas erupt on to the surface of the earth. The world's highest active volcano is Volcan Antofalla 6,100 m (20,015 ft) in Argentina. The highest extinct volcano is Cerro Aconcagua, 6,960 m (22,835 ft) also in Argentina.

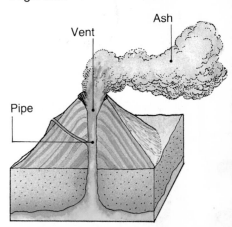

Ash

Vent

Pipe

Index